This Planner Belongs To:

....

....

....

Weekly Meal Planner

Week of............	Breakfast	Lunch	Dinner
Monday			
Tuesday			
Wednesday			
Thursday			
Friday			
Saturday			
Sunday			

	Snacks	Shopping List	
Monday	....	....	....
Tuesday	....	....	....
Wednesday	....	....	....
Thursday	....	....	....
Friday	....	....	....
Saturday	....	....	....
Sunday	....	....	....

Weekly Meal Planner

Week of............................	Breakfast	Lunch	Dinner
Monday			
Tuesday			
Wednesday			
Thursday			
Friday			
Saturday			
Sunday			

	Snacks	Shopping List
Monday	....	....
Tuesday	....	....
Wednesday	....	....
Thursday	....	....
Friday	....	....
Saturday	....	....
Sunday	....	....

Weekly Meal Planner

Week of....................	Breakfast	Lunch	Dinner
Monday			
Tuesday			
Wednesday			
Thursday			
Friday			
Saturday			
Sunday			

	Snacks	Shopping List
Monday	....	....
Tuesday	....	....
Wednesday	....	....
Thursday	....	....
Friday	....	....
Saturday	....	....
Sunday	....	....

Weekly Meal Planner

Week of..............	Breakfast	Lunch	Dinner
Monday			
Tuesday			
Wednesday			
Thursday			
Friday			
Saturday			
Sunday			

	Snacks	Shopping List	
Monday	....	....	....
	....	....	....
	....	....	....
Tuesday	....	....	....
	....	....	....
	....	....	....
Wednesday	....	....	....
	....	....	....
	....	....	....
Thursday	....	....	....
	....	....	....
	....	....	....
Friday	....	....	....
	....	....	....
	....	....	....
Saturday	....	....	....
	....	....	....
	....	....	....
Sunday	....	....	....
	....	....	....
	....	....	....

Weekly Meal Planner

Week of	Breakfast	Lunch	Dinner
Monday			
Tuesday			
Wednesday			
Thursday			
Friday			
Saturday			
Sunday			

	Snacks	Shopping List	
Monday	....	....	....
	....	....	....
	....	....	....
Tuesday	....	....	....
	....	....	....
	....	....	....
Wednesday	....	....	....
	....	....	....
	....	....	....
Thursday	....	....	....
	....	....	....
	....	....	....
Friday	....	....	....
	....	....	....
	....	....	....
Saturday	....	....	....
	....	....	....
	....	....	....
Sunday	....	....	....
	....	....	....
	....	....	....

Weekly Meal Planner

Week of	Breakfast	Lunch	Dinner
Monday			
Tuesday			
Wednesday			
Thursday			
Friday			
Saturday			
Sunday			

	Snacks	Shopping List
Monday	....	....
Tuesday	....	....
Wednesday	....	....
Thursday	....	....
Friday	....	....
Saturday	....	....
Sunday	....	....

Weekly Meal Planner

Week of............	Breakfast	Lunch	Dinner
Monday			
Tuesday			
Wednesday			
Thursday			
Friday			
Saturday			
Sunday			

	Snacks	Shopping List
Monday	....	....
	....	....
	....	....
Tuesday	....	....
	....	....
	....	....
Wednesday	....	....
	....	....
	....	....
Thursday	....	....
	....	....
	....	....
Friday	....	....
	....	....
	....	....
Saturday	....	....
	....	....
	....	....
Sunday	....	....
	....	....
	....	....

Weekly Meal Planner

Week of	Breakfast	Lunch	Dinner
Monday			
Tuesday			
Wednesday			
Thursday			
Friday			
Saturday			
Sunday			

	Snacks	Shopping List
Monday	....	....
Tuesday	....	....
Wednesday	....	....
Thursday	....	....
Friday	....	....
Saturday	....	....
Sunday	....	....

Weekly Meal Planner

Week of...............	Breakfast	Lunch	Dinner
Monday			
Tuesday			
Wednesday			
Thursday			
Friday			
Saturday			
Sunday			

	Snacks	Shopping List
Monday	....	....	....
Tuesday	....	....	....
Wednesday	....	....	....
Thursday	....	....	....
Friday	....	....	....
Saturday	....	....	....
Sunday	....	....	....

Weekly Meal Planner

Week of........................	Breakfast	Lunch	Dinner
Monday			
Tuesday			
Wednesday			
Thursday			
Friday			
Saturday			
Sunday			

	Snacks	Shopping List	
Monday	....	....	....
Tuesday	....	....	....
Wednesday	....	....	....
Thursday	....	....	....
Friday	....	....	....
Saturday	....	....	....
Sunday	....	....	....

Weekly Meal Planner

Week of...............	Breakfast	Lunch	Dinner
Monday			
Tuesday			
Wednesday			
Thursday			
Friday			
Saturday			
Sunday			

	Snacks	Shopping List
Monday	....	....
Tuesday	....	....
Wednesday	....	....
Thursday	....	....
Friday	....	....
Saturday	....	....
Sunday	....	....

Weekly Meal Planner

Week of............	Breakfast	Lunch	Dinner
Monday			
Tuesday			
Wednesday			
Thursday			
Friday			
Saturday			
Sunday			

	Snacks	Shopping List	
Monday			
Tuesday			
Wednesday			
Thursday			
Friday			
Saturday			
Sunday			

Weekly Meal Planner

Week of....................	Breakfast	Lunch	Dinner
Monday			
Tuesday			
Wednesday			
Thursday			
Friday			
Saturday			
Sunday			

	Snacks	Shopping List
Monday		
Tuesday		
Wednesday		
Thursday		
Friday		
Saturday		
Sunday		

Weekly Meal Planner

Week of............	Breakfast	Lunch	Dinner
Monday			
Tuesday			
Wednesday			
Thursday			
Friday			
Saturday			
Sunday			

	Snacks	Shopping List	
Monday	....	....	....
Tuesday	....	....	....
Wednesday	....	....	....
Thursday	....	....	....
Friday	....	....	....
Saturday	....	....	....
Sunday	....	....	....

Weekly Meal Planner

Week of...............	Breakfast	Lunch	Dinner
Monday			
Tuesday			
Wednesday			
Thursday			
Friday			
Saturday			
Sunday			

	Snacks	Shopping List	
Monday	....	....	....
	....	....	....
	....	....	....
Tuesday	....	....	....
	....	....	....
	....	....	....
Wednesday	....	....	....
	....	....	....
	....	....	....
Thursday	....	....	....
	....	....	....
	....	....	....
Friday	....	....	....
	....	....	....
	....	....	....
Saturday	....	....	....
	....	....	....
	....	....	....
Sunday	....	....	....
	....	....	....
	....	....	....

Weekly Meal Planner

Week of...............	Breakfast	Lunch	Dinner
Monday	....	....	....
Tuesday	....	....	....
Wednesday	....	....	....
Thursday	....	....	....
Friday	....	....	....
Saturday	....	....	....
Sunday	....	....	....

	Snacks	Shopping List	
Monday	....	....	....
Tuesday	....	....	....
Wednesday	....	....	....
Thursday	....	....	....
Friday	....	....	....
Saturday	....	....	....
Sunday	....	....	....

Weekly Meal Planner

Week of...............	Breakfast	Lunch	Dinner
Monday			
Tuesday			
Wednesday			
Thursday			
Friday			
Saturday			
Sunday			

	Snacks	Shopping List	
Monday	....	....	....
	....	....	....
	....	....	....
Tuesday	....	....	....
	....	....	....
	....	....	....
Wednesday	....	....	....
	....	....	....
	....	....	....
Thursday	....	....	....
	....	....	....
	....	....	....
Friday	....	....	....
	....	....	....
	....	....	....
Saturday	....	....	....
	....	....	....
	....	....	....
Sunday	....	....	....
	....	....	....
	....	....	....

Weekly Meal Planner

Week of............	Breakfast	Lunch	Dinner
Monday			
Tuesday			
Wednesday			
Thursday			
Friday			
Saturday			
Sunday			

	Snacks	Shopping List	
Monday	....	....	....
Tuesday	....	....	....
Wednesday	....	....	....
Thursday	....	....	....
Friday	....	....	....
Saturday	....	....	....
Sunday	....	....	....

Weekly Meal Planner

Week of.............	Breakfast	Lunch	Dinner
Monday			
Tuesday			
Wednesday			
Thursday			
Friday			
Saturday			
Sunday			

	Snacks	Shopping List
Monday	....	....
Tuesday	....	....
Wednesday	....	....
Thursday	....	....
Friday	....	....
Saturday	....	....
Sunday	....	....

Weekly Meal Planner

Week of............	Breakfast	Lunch	Dinner
Monday			
Tuesday			
Wednesday			
Thursday			
Friday			
Saturday			
Sunday			

	Snacks	Shopping List	
Monday	....	....	....
Tuesday	....	....	....
Wednesday	....	....	....
Thursday	....	....	....
Friday	....	....	....
Saturday	....	....	....
Sunday	....	....	....

Weekly Meal Planner

Week of............................	Breakfast	Lunch	Dinner
Monday	....	....	....
Tuesday	....	....	....
Wednesday	....	....	....
Thursday	....	....	....
Friday	....	....	....
Saturday	....	....	....
Sunday	....	....	....

	Snacks	Shopping List
Monday	....	....
Tuesday	....	....
Wednesday	....	....
Thursday	....	....
Friday	....	....
Saturday	....	....
Sunday	....	....

Weekly Meal Planner

Week of..................	Breakfast	Lunch	Dinner
Monday			
Tuesday			
Wednesday			
Thursday			
Friday			
Saturday			
Sunday			

	Snacks	Shopping List	
Monday	....	....	....
	....	....	....
	....	....	....
Tuesday	....	....	....
	....	....	....
	....	....	....
Wednesday	....	....	....
	....	....	....
	....	....	....
Thursday	....	....	....
	....	....	....
	....	....	....
Friday	....	....	....
	....	....	....
	....	....	....
Saturday	....	....	....
	....	....	....
	....	....	....
Sunday	....	....	....
	....	....	....
	....	....	....

Weekly Meal Planner

Week of..................	Breakfast	Lunch	Dinner
Monday			
Tuesday			
Wednesday			
Thursday			
Friday			
Saturday			
Sunday			

	Snacks	Shopping List	
Monday	....	....	....
Tuesday	....	....	....
Wednesday	....	....	....
Thursday	....	....	....
Friday	....	....	....
Saturday	....	....	....
Sunday	....	....	....

Weekly Meal Planner

Week of...............	Breakfast	Lunch	Dinner
Monday			
Tuesday			
Wednesday			
Thursday			
Friday			
Saturday			
Sunday			

	Snacks	Shopping List
Monday		
Tuesday		
Wednesday		
Thursday		
Friday		
Saturday		
Sunday		

Weekly Meal Planner

Week of...............	Breakfast	Lunch	Dinner
Monday			
Tuesday			
Wednesday			
Thursday			
Friday			
Saturday			
Sunday			

	Snacks	Shopping List	
Monday	....	....	....
Tuesday	....	....	....
Wednesday	....	....	....
Thursday	....	....	....
Friday	....	....	....
Saturday	....	....	....
Sunday	....	....	....

Weekly Meal Planner

Week of................	Breakfast	Lunch	Dinner
Monday			
Tuesday			
Wednesday			
Thursday			
Friday			
Saturday			
Sunday			

	Snacks	Shopping List
Monday		
Tuesday		
Wednesday		
Thursday		
Friday		
Saturday		
Sunday		

Weekly Meal Planner

Week of..........................	Breakfast	Lunch	Dinner
Monday			
Tuesday			
Wednesday			
Thursday			
Friday			
Saturday			
Sunday			

	Snacks	Shopping List
Monday	....	....	....
Tuesday	....	....	....
Wednesday	....	....	....
Thursday	....	....	....
Friday	....	....	....
Saturday	....	....	....
Sunday	....	....	....

Weekly Meal Planner

Week of	Breakfast	Lunch	Dinner
Monday			
Tuesday			
Wednesday			
Thursday			
Friday			
Saturday			
Sunday			

	Snacks	Shopping List	
Monday	....	....	....
Tuesday	....	....	....
Wednesday	....	....	....
Thursday	....	....	....
Friday	....	....	....
Saturday	....	....	....
Sunday	....	....	....

Weekly Meal Planner

Week of............	Breakfast	Lunch	Dinner
Monday			
Tuesday			
Wednesday			
Thursday			
Friday			
Saturday			
Sunday			

	Snacks	Shopping List	
Monday	....	....	....
Tuesday	....	....	....
Wednesday	....	....	....
Thursday	....	....	....
Friday	....	....	....
Saturday	....	....	....
Sunday	....	....	....

Weekly Meal Planner

Week of............	Breakfast	Lunch	Dinner
Monday	....	....	....
Tuesday	....	....	....
Wednesday	....	....	....
Thursday	....	....	....
Friday	....	....	....
Saturday	....	....	....
Sunday	....	....	....

	Snacks	Shopping List	
Monday			
Tuesday			
Wednesday			
Thursday			
Friday			
Saturday			
Sunday			

Weekly Meal Planner

Week of...............	Breakfast	Lunch	Dinner
Monday			
Tuesday			
Wednesday			
Thursday			
Friday			
Saturday			
Sunday			

	Snacks	Shopping List
Monday		
Tuesday		
Wednesday		
Thursday		
Friday		
Saturday		
Sunday		

Weekly Meal Planner

Week of...............	Breakfast	Lunch	Dinner
Monday			
Tuesday			
Wednesday			
Thursday			
Friday			
Saturday			
Sunday			

	Snacks	Shopping List
Monday	....	....
Tuesday	....	....
Wednesday	....	....
Thursday	....	....
Friday	....	....
Saturday	....	....
Sunday	....	....

Weekly Meal Planner

Week of...............	Breakfast	Lunch	Dinner
Monday			
Tuesday			
Wednesday			
Thursday			
Friday			
Saturday			
Sunday			

	Snacks	Shopping List	
Monday	....	....	....
Tuesday	....	....	....
Wednesday	....	....	....
Thursday	....	....	....
Friday	....	....	....
Saturday	....	....	....
Sunday	....	....	....

Weekly Meal Planner

Week of...............	Breakfast	Lunch	Dinner
Monday			
Tuesday			
Wednesday			
Thursday			
Friday			
Saturday			
Sunday			

	Snacks	Shopping List	
Monday	....	....	....
Tuesday	....	....	....
Wednesday	....	....	....
Thursday	....	....	....
Friday	....	....	....
Saturday	....	....	....
Sunday	....	....	....

Weekly Meal Planner

Week of.............................	Breakfast	Lunch	Dinner
Monday			
Tuesday			
Wednesday			
Thursday			
Friday			
Saturday			
Sunday			

	Snacks	Shopping List
Monday	....	....
Tuesday	....	....
Wednesday	....	....
Thursday	....	....
Friday	....	....
Saturday	....	....
Sunday	....	....

Weekly Meal Planner

Week of	Breakfast	Lunch	Dinner
Monday			
Tuesday			
Wednesday			
Thursday			
Friday			
Saturday			
Sunday			

	Snacks	Shopping List
Monday	....	....
Tuesday	....	....
Wednesday	....	....
Thursday	....	....
Friday	....	....
Saturday	....	....
Sunday	....	....

Weekly Meal Planner

Week of..................	Breakfast	Lunch	Dinner
Monday			
Tuesday			
Wednesday			
Thursday			
Friday			
Saturday			
Sunday			

	Snacks	Shopping List	
Monday			
Tuesday			
Wednesday			
Thursday			
Friday			
Saturday			
Sunday			

Weekly Meal Planner

Week of............................	Breakfast	Lunch	Dinner
Monday			
Tuesday			
Wednesday			
Thursday			
Friday			
Saturday			
Sunday			

	Snacks	Shopping List	
Monday	....	....	....
Tuesday	....	....	....
Wednesday	....	....	....
Thursday	....	....	....
Friday	....	....	....
Saturday	....	....	....
Sunday	....	....	....

Weekly Meal Planner

Week of............	Breakfast	Lunch	Dinner
Monday			
Tuesday			
Wednesday			
Thursday			
Friday			
Saturday			
Sunday			

	Snacks	Shopping List	
Monday	....	....	....
Tuesday	....	....	....
Wednesday	....	....	....
Thursday	....	....	....
Friday	....	....	....
Saturday	....	....	....
Sunday	....	....	....

Weekly Meal Planner

Week of............	Breakfast	Lunch	Dinner
Monday			
Tuesday			
Wednesday			
Thursday			
Friday			
Saturday			
Sunday			

	Snacks	Shopping List	
Monday			
Tuesday			
Wednesday			
Thursday			
Friday			
Saturday			
Sunday			

Weekly Meal Planner

Week of............	Breakfast	Lunch	Dinner
Monday			
Tuesday			
Wednesday			
Thursday			
Friday			
Saturday			
Sunday			

	Snacks	Shopping List	
Monday	....	....	....
Tuesday	....	....	....
Wednesday	....	....	....
Thursday	....	....	....
Friday	....	....	....
Saturday	....	....	....
Sunday	....	....	....

Weekly Meal Planner

Week of............................	Breakfast	Lunch	Dinner
Monday			
Tuesday			
Wednesday			
Thursday			
Friday			
Saturday			
Sunday			

	Snacks	Shopping List	
Monday	....	....	....
Tuesday	....	....	....
Wednesday	....	....	....
Thursday	....	....	....
Friday	....	....	....
Saturday	....	....	....
Sunday	....	....	....

Weekly Meal Planner

Week of............	Breakfast	Lunch	Dinner
Monday			
Tuesday			
Wednesday			
Thursday			
Friday			
Saturday			
Sunday			

	Snacks	Shopping List	
Monday	....	....	....
	....	....	....
	....	....	....
Tuesday	....	....	....
	....	....	....
	....	....	....
Wednesday	....	....	....
	....	....	....
	....	....	....
Thursday	....	....	....
	....	....	....
	....	....	....
Friday	....	....	....
	....	....	....
	....	....	....
Saturday	....	....	....
	....	....	....
	....	....	....
Sunday	....	....	....
	....	....	....
	....	....	....

Weekly Meal Planner

Week of.............	Breakfast	Lunch	Dinner
Monday			
Tuesday			
Wednesday			
Thursday			
Friday			
Saturday			
Sunday			

	Snacks	Shopping List	
Monday	....	....	....
Tuesday	....	....	....
Wednesday	....	....	....
Thursday	....	....	....
Friday	....	....	....
Saturday	....	....	....
Sunday	....	....	....

Weekly Meal Planner

Week of................	Breakfast	Lunch	Dinner
Monday			
Tuesday			
Wednesday			
Thursday			
Friday			
Saturday			
Sunday			

	Snacks	Shopping List
Monday	....	....
Tuesday	....	....
Wednesday	....	....
Thursday	....	....
Friday	....	....
Saturday	....	....
Sunday	....	....

Weekly Meal Planner

Week of........................	Breakfast	Lunch	Dinner
Monday			
Tuesday			
Wednesday			
Thursday			
Friday			
Saturday			
Sunday			

	Snacks	Shopping List	
Monday			
Tuesday			
Wednesday			
Thursday			
Friday			
Saturday			
Sunday			

Weekly Meal Planner

Week of................	Breakfast	Lunch	Dinner
Monday			
Tuesday			
Wednesday			
Thursday			
Friday			
Saturday			
Sunday			

	Snacks	Shopping List	
Monday	....	....	....
Tuesday	....	....	....
Wednesday	....	....	....
Thursday	....	....	....
Friday	....	....	....
Saturday	....	....	....
Sunday	....	....	....

Weekly Meal Planner

Week of..............	Breakfast	Lunch	Dinner
Monday			
Tuesday			
Wednesday			
Thursday			
Friday			
Saturday			
Sunday			

	Snacks	Shopping List	
Monday	....	....	....
	....	....	....
	....	....	....
Tuesday	....	....	....
	....	....	....
	....	....	....
Wednesday	....	....	....
	....	....	....
	....	....	....
Thursday	....	....	....
	....	....	....
	....	....	....
Friday	....	....	....
	....	....	....
	....	....	....
Saturday	....	....	....
	....	....	....
	....	....	....
Sunday	....	....	....
	....	....	....
	....	....	....

Weekly Meal Planner

Week of........................	Breakfast	Lunch	Dinner
Monday			
Tuesday			
Wednesday			
Thursday			
Friday			
Saturday			
Sunday			

	Snacks	Shopping List
Monday		
Tuesday		
Wednesday		
Thursday		
Friday		
Saturday		
Sunday		

Weekly Meal Planner

Week of....................	Breakfast	Lunch	Dinner
Monday			
Tuesday			
Wednesday			
Thursday			
Friday			
Saturday			
Sunday			

	Snacks	Shopping List	
Monday	....	....	....
Tuesday	....	....	....
Wednesday	....	....	....
Thursday	....	....	....
Friday	....	....	....
Saturday	....	....	....
Sunday	....	....	....

Weekly Meal Planner

Week of...............	Breakfast	Lunch	Dinner
Monday			
Tuesday			
Wednesday			
Thursday			
Friday			
Saturday			
Sunday			

	Snacks	Shopping List	
Monday	....	....	....
	....	....	....
	....	....	....
Tuesday	....	....	....
	....	....	....
	....	....	....
Wednesday	....	....	....
	....	....	....
	....	....	....
Thursday	....	....	....
	....	....	....
	....	....	....
Friday	....	....	....
	....	....	....
	....	....	....
Saturday	....	....	....
	....	....	....
	....	....	....
Sunday	....	....	....
	....	....	....
	....	....	....

Weekly Meal Planner

Week of............	Breakfast	Lunch	Dinner
Monday			
Tuesday			
Wednesday			
Thursday			
Friday			
Saturday			
Sunday			

	Snacks	Shopping List	
Monday			
Tuesday			
Wednesday			
Thursday			
Friday			
Saturday			
Sunday			

Weekly Meal Planner

Week of.............................	Breakfast	Lunch	Dinner
Monday			
Tuesday			
Wednesday			
Thursday			
Friday			
Saturday			
Sunday			

	Snacks	Shopping List	
Monday	....	....	....
Tuesday	....	....	....
Wednesday	....	....	....
Thursday	....	....	....
Friday	....	....	....
Saturday	....	....	....
Sunday	....	....	....

Weekly Meal Planner

Week of...............	Breakfast	Lunch	Dinner
Monday			
Tuesday			
Wednesday			
Thursday			
Friday			
Saturday			
Sunday			

	Snacks	Shopping List	
Monday	....	....	....
Tuesday	....	....	....
Wednesday	....	....	....
Thursday	....	....	....
Friday	....	....	....
Saturday	....	....	....
Sunday	....	....	....

Weekly Meal Planner

Week of..........................	Breakfast	Lunch	Dinner
Monday			
Tuesday			
Wednesday			
Thursday			
Friday			
Saturday			
Sunday			

	Snacks	Shopping List	
Monday	....	....	....
Tuesday	....	....	....
Wednesday	....	....	....
Thursday	....	....	....
Friday	....	....	....
Saturday	....	....	....
Sunday	....	....	....

Recipe

Ingredients

Prep time:

Cook time:

Serving:

Date:

Directions:

Recipe

Ingredients

Prep time: **Cook time:**

Serving: **Date:**

Directions:

Recipe

Ingredients

Prep time:

Cook time:

Serving:

Date:

Directions:

Recipe

Ingredients

Prep time: Cook time:

Serving: Date:

Directions:

Recipe

Ingredients

Prep time:

Cook time:

Serving:

Date:

Directions:

Recipe

Ingredients

Prep time: **Cook time:**

Serving: **Date:**

Directions:

Recipe

Ingredients

Prep time:

Cook time:

Serving:

Date:

Directions:

Recipe

Ingredients

Prep time: **Cook time:**

Serving: **Date:**

Directions:

Made in the USA
Las Vegas, NV
21 April 2021